This book is dedicated to my Uncles who are retired Ministers:

Reverend Joseph Pitts
Reverend Samuel Pitts

May God bless their work of labor and love.

THE MILEAGE
THE MESSAGE
THE MESS

by Nolan T. Pitts

Unless otherwise noted, all Scripture quotations are from the King James Version of the Bible. Personal emphasis, noted by italics, has also been added in various verses.

Published by:
Longwood Communications
397 Kingslake Drive
DeBary, FL 32713
904-774-1991

CONTENTS

Acknowledgements 7
Preface 10

1   Abram Obeys on a Promise 14
2   Moses Sent on a Messy Mission..............21
3   Jonah Angry About God's Mercy 32
4   God's Odd Couple................................37
5   Tears of Jeremiah 40
6   A Moving Testimony 43
7   Saul Spiritually Arrested.......................48
8   Only Faithfulness is Required.................54
9   Don't Ever Laugh at God 59
10 Mess Hold Us in Check 62
11 Contemporary Mess 64
12 Human Wrecks 68
13 Mess Among the Ministerial Ranks 71
14 Mileage and Mess in Marriages 76
15 Grapes From the Vine 84
    Resources 90

ACKNOWLEDGEMENTS

I am grateful to have had at my disposal the various resources that have aided me in formulating and writing this book. I am also thankful to the pastors with whom I have communicated for sharing some of their experiences.

A special thanks to Mildred Williams for her patience, time and talent in typing this material, and to Shirley Baker for her editing skills.

Above all I thank God for the privilege and presence of the Holy Spirit in my life. I thank my family for allowing me the solitude to expend my innermost thoughts and concerns.

Nolan T. Pitts

And ye shall be hated of all men for my name's sake; but he that endureth to the end shall be saved. Matthew 10:22

Any human being who observes nature, the precision of the planets, and declares that there is no God should be classified as a **certified fool**. It does not take a genius to recognize that this world's existence is not a mere accident. And if it were, the accident had to be caused by somebody or something. Behind every movement is a mover. Nothing moves unless it is compelled, propelled or attracted by another force.

How often do we make references to the "hands of God" and the "eyes of God"? God Almighty does not have arms, legs, fingers, muscles or eyes. God is not flesh and blood; He is a spirit. We all are more spiritual than physical. We respond to God in the spirit. We are housed in a cloak of clay only for identification to one another. If this were not so, all of us would look alike. God is so divine that he even gave each of us a different set of fingerprints.

How much more intelligent can He be? Out of all the people who have been born in this world, there has never been and never will be a duplication of fingerprints. How great God is! And yet there are those who declare that there is no God. How can a person admire a design without considering the designer? If he can, he stands in absolute ignorance. Skyscrapers, bridges and massive domes are all works of architects and builders. So why should the earth in all its splendor be attributed to anything less than the genius of a great designer?

As a child, I had many questions concerning the world and its existence. Those questions now seem a little silly, but then they were not.

There are many questions that are never asked because we fear embarrassment. Some of the questions I asked were: What was here before the world was formed? Was there ever a time when there was nothing? If so, how did nothing become something when there was nothing to make something? Why can't I see the wind? Where do the stars go after dark? I am sure that by now you agree with me that these sound like silly questions, but back then they were not.

Being curious is a good and natural thing. It is the only way we can find answers. Scientists call it research because they have a methodology by which to ascertain information. Even now scientists are constantly probing the universe in search of "intelligent life." However, I am not sure what we call intelligent. Life in any form, earthling or alien, is an intelligent form created by God.

The inspiration and title of this book are not without firm foundation.This world in which we live is a world of motion. Everything, whether human, animal, natural, celestial or terrestrial moves.

The planets move with the precision of the mechanisms of a grandfather clock. People move, genes and chromosomes move, earth and wind move, oceans and rivers move. God is a God of action; He speaks, and things move.In the book of Genesis we read that God said, "Let there be light; and there was light." And God said, "Let there be a firmament in the midst of the waters, and let it divide the waters from the waters." God said, "Let the waters under the heaven be gathered together unto one place and it was so."

And then God said, "Let the earth bring forth grass, the herb yielding seed, and the fruit tree yielding fruit after its kind, whose seed is in itself, upon the earth: and it was so." When God speaks, creation moves.The following scriptures were the inspiration for the title of this book:

> Go ye therefore and teach all nations, baptizing
> them in the name of the Father, the son and the
> Holy Ghost. Matthew 28:19

> Behold, I send ye forth as sheep in the midst of
> wolves, be ye therefore wise as serpents and
> harmless as doves. Matthew 10:16

> But beware of men, for they will deliver you up
> to the councils and they will scourge you in their
> synagogues. Matthew 10:17

Let us look at the words go, teach, send, wolves and scourge. To go suggests mileage. This is not only physical movement but also spiritual movement. We cannot go if we are standing still. And when we go we are to teach all nations, which means we must travel and not be satisfied by staying in our own communities. If we are to teach, there must be a message. However, if no message is given us, then we have no message to teach others.

Jesus said, "They will scourge you." This is where the

mess comes. To be scourged means to be punished severely, inflicted with pain and made to suffer. The pain is not only physical, it is in many cases psychological and emotional. The "mess" will leave physical scars or unseen scars that zap the very spirit out of each of us.

It was Paul who said, "I bear in my body the marks [scars] of the Lord Jesus." There will be scars, but we can and will overcome them if we are grounded in the Word.

This book, *The Mileage, The Message and The Mess*, is not written to discourage anyone from accepting the call, but rather to create an awareness that the road to witnessing is never promised to be easy. If you are a messenger for Christ, never expect to be popular. And, if you are sincere about the work of the Lord, never expect to be rich. There are many of us in missions whose search for riches contributes to the creation of the mess.

I hope and pray that this book will enlighten but not frighten you. How often we sing about the "rough side of the mountain." I thank God for the rough side, for it is far more difficult to climb a smooth mountain. Nothing to hold on to, nothing to grasp, and nothing to stand on. Nothing to use as stepping stones. The mess we will encounter will become footholds on the mountain—helping us achieve that crown which is promised. May reading this book give you renewed hope in your work for Christ.

CHAPTER 1

Abram Obeys on a Promise

There was a man named Abram who with his wife Sarai was living comfortably on his father's estate; his father was an idolater. God spoke to Abram and instructed him to get out of the country, away from his kinfolk, and to a land that God had selected. God promised Abram that his name would be great and that he would become the father of a great nation. Abram had to put in the mileage; he had to leave his homeland. God told Abram that not only would he bless him, he would also bless those who blessed him and curse those who cursed him. Having been made aware of bad times ahead, Abram, ready for some "mess," went to Sarai to break the news to her. Permit me to imagine what could have taken place in a dialogue between Abram and Sarai:

Abram: Sarai, get up and get our things together. We

are leaving this country.

Sarai: Where are we going, Abram?

Abram: I don't know; just get the things together.

Sarai: Abram, you are seventy-five years old, and you come in here telling me to get the things together and that we are leaving, and you don't know where we are going? Are you out of your mind?

Abram: I am not out of my mind; just get the things together.

Sarai: Why are we leaving?

Abram: Because God told me to go.

Sarai: Which one? What God?

We must understand that, living in a polytheistic society, this was a very logical question. There is no record of how long it took Abram to respond to God's instruction, but we do know he took his wife Sarai, his nephew Lot, and all his possessions and left for the land of promise. We must take note that for a person living in a polytheistic society, and also in a household that practiced idolatry, to be singled out by God and chosen to be blessed was an awesome privilege. Abram was not a prophet, but what God was going to do for him and with him was a message to the world. But I am sure Abram had no idea what awaited him on the way to the promised land.

It took Abram about ten years to reach the land of promise, for on the way he encountered quite a mess. As he journeyed southward, there was a famine in the land, and Abram went into Egypt to find food. This was the first mess: Abram had to lie about his wife Sarai because he realized that if the Egyptians knew that she, a beautiful woman even at age sixty-five, was his wife, they would take her and kill him. So Abram lied and said Sarai was his sister.

However, in reality Abram did not lie. You see, Sarai

was Abram's half sister. She was the daughter of Abram's father Terah. Abram did what he had to do to get himself out of the mess he was in. Later, when Pharoah discovered the truth about Abram, he admonished him for his conduct and sent Abram away with all of his possessions. I am almost certain that Abram had many second thoughts about his mission to go to a strange land which he knew not.

The next mess came in the form of a family feud. Abram's nephew Lot had trouble with the herdsmen of Abram. Both of them had increased in their possessions— their cattle, sheep and so forth. The land on which they now dwelt was not able to sustain both of their herds. No mess is like the mess within a family. Abram was conciliatory: He gave Lot the opportunity to choose which land he wanted.

Lot chose the fertile plain of Jordan, and Abram occupied the land of Canaan, where he settled. God kept His promise. He told Abram to look north, east, south and west, and whatever he saw was his. In other words, "what you see is what you get." God promised to make Abram's seed as the dust of the earth, which meant that it would be impossible to number.

Abram was getting old, and Sarai was past child-bearing age. I am sure that Abram was concerned about the "promise seed" which God had said He would bless and multiply. "I will multiply thy seed as the dust of the earth." Many times we become anxious to fulfill those things which are promised. Sarai wanted to assure Abram that he would have heirs to bring to reality what God had promised. She commanded her maid, Hagar, to go in and "know" Abram. As all slaves were expected to do, Hagar went in to Abram. I don't know whether or not Sarai expected any positive results, but we must realize that in those days, and even now in some places, it was humiliating for a woman not to be able to bear children. As a result of the mating, Hagar became pregnant, and this is where much more mess started. Here is where Abram became a victim of circumstance. Sarai became furiously angry. I believe she had a serious problem with herself. She considered herself inferior especially in the eyes of the slave, Hagar.

Sarai: Abram, this is all your fault. Hagar despises me, and I am the one who gave her the privilege of "knowing" you. I hope God punishes you for this.

Abram: Sarai, the girl is your servant, and you have the right to do whatever you want to her. You have my blessing.

Sarai beat and scolded Hagar terribly—so much so that Hagar fled for her life. Keep in mind that Abram was ninety-six years old when he impregnated Hagar.

There was no romance between Abram and Hagar, just an obedient slave and a willing Abram. I think even Abram was surprised at the outcome of this mating. But he really wanted an heir to fulfill the promise of God.

Abram was deeply concerned because he did not have a lawful heir. God told Abram if he walked before Him and was perfect, the covenant He had made would be fulfilled. God changed Abram's name to Abraham, and Sarai's name to Sarah. God told Sarah that she would become a mother of nations. Abraham did something we must never do. Abraham fell to the ground laughing at God. Abraham laughed because he knew that Sarah was far past the child-bearing age. He was one hundred and Sarah was ninety. Angels brought the message to Sarah, and she laughed also. God questioned Sarah about her laughter, but Sarah tried to deny it. She must not have known that God is omniscient. Sarah did become pregnant, and her illegitimate son, Ishmael, made fun of her condition. He laughed her to scorn. This made Sarah furious, and the mess started up again. These were difficult times for Abraham.

Sarah: Abraham! Throw this slave woman out!
Abraham: Why do you want to throw her out?
Sarah: Her son, Ishmael, made mockery of me, and furthermore he will not be an heir with my son.

God spoke to Abraham and told him not to worry about his son, Ishmael. "Do what Sarah wants and let them go. This was a mess to put your own blood to flight." I wonder what was going on in Abraham's mind as he got up early and prepared to send his own flesh and blood out into the desert. I know, being human, that Abraham had a restless night. Abraham took a bottle of water and some bread and placed it on Hagar's shoulder and sent them away to wander in the wilderness. More mess to come.

After Abraham had stood and witnessed the destruction of the cities of Sodom and Gomorrah, he left the plains of Mamre and traveled south and settled in a town called Gerar. And here again he had to lie concerning his wife Sarah. He was afraid that King Abimelech would take her for his own. But God spoke to Abimelech in a dream and warned him of the situation. The king confronted Abraham and Abraham tried to justify what he had done. Abraham was doing what he thought was right in his heart. He thought that the people who lived in this town were not God-fearing, but he was wrong. Abimelech was very generous to Abraham and gave him sheep, oxen and servants, men and women, and also gave him back his wife. Abraham did well and prospered with his sheep and oxen.

Abimelech: Abraham! God has been good to you and

has blessed you in everything you have done.

Abraham: Yes, God has been very good to me.

Abimelech: Will you promise me that you will not defraud me nor my son nor my grandson, and will you swear before God that you will be friends with my country as I have been to yours?

Abraham: But, Abimelech! One of your servants stole one of my wells.

Abimelech: Abraham! I don't know anything about that. Why didn't you tell me about that before now? I would have done something about it.

The mess was not over. Sarah gave birth to a son and called him Isaac. This was to be a testing time for Abraham.

God: Abraham!

Abraham: Here I am, Lord.

God: Abraham! Take your son Isaac into the land of Moriah and prepare him for a burnt offering. It will be on one of the mountains. I will show you when the time comes.

As before, Abraham obeyed the voice of God. Imagine his having to offer his only son as a burnt offering. What strong faith! What unfaltering obedience!

Abraham: Isaac, come with me to the mountain to offer a sacrifice.

Isaac: Father, we have the wood in place, and the fire is ready; where is the offering?

Abraham: Don't worry, son, God will provide.

Isaac: Father, why are you binding me up? Where is the offering?

After making ready his son, Abraham took a knife and raised his hand to kill Isaac.

Angel of the Lord: Abraham! Abraham!
Abraham: Here am I.
Angel of the Lord: Don't do any harm to your son. God has tested you and now knows that you are a God-fearing man.

I don't know anyone today who can testify to such a litany of "mess" as Abraham endured.

Abraham proved his faith, just as we today must prove our faith. We must put our complete trust in God and know that He will provide. Abraham had experienced the whole nine yards: The Mileage, the Message and the Mess.

And Moses answered and said, But behold, they
will not believe me, nor hearken unto my voice;
for they will say, The Lord hath not appeared
unto thee. Exodus 4:1

CHAPTER 2

Moses Sent on a Messy Mission

Out on the backside of the Arabian mountains, there was a man named Moses tending his flock when an unusual sight caught his eyes. He saw a bush burning furiously but not being consumed by the fire. Obviously this would cause anyone some curiosity. Moses said, "I will now turn aside, and see this great sight, why the bush is not burnt." God used the bush to get Moses' attention. God could not speak to him until he turned aside from the daily routine of life. There are many ways by which God tries to get our attention, but we are so busy with the hum-drum of daily routine that we fail to be curious. We may not have the opportunity to see a bush on fire, but there are other activities that demand our attention.

As Moses approached the bush, he heard a voice speaking from the flame. Let me first say that Moses was a fugitive from justice. He had murdered an Egyptian for flogging a Hebrew. This bush was the method God used to bring Moses into His presence.

> **God:** Moses, stop where you are and take off your shoes, for the ground on which you are standing is holy.

Moses was awed by such a sight and was so startled by the communication that he hid his face from God, not in shame but in humility. God told Moses that He had heard the cries of the children in bondage down in Egypt. He had seen their suffering at the hands of their taskmasters. God told Moses that He was sending him unto Pharaoh with a message, and that message was, "Let my people go." Moses had to go to Egypt (mileage), he had to tell Pharoah what God had said (message), but little did Moses know that he was in for a lot of trouble (the mess).

> **Moses:** Who am I that I should confront Pharaoh? Who am I that I am chosen to bring the children out of Egypt?
>
> **God:** Moses! I will be with you.
>
> **Moses:** When I come to the children and tell them that the God of their Fathers sent me, what shall I say to them?

Moses wanted to know how he was going to explain which "god" sent him. Remember, he was the product of a polytheistic society. Moses wanted to be sure of the true identity of this God with such authority. God said to Moses, "Tell them, '*I am that I am* hath sent me.'" God gave Moses a blank identification. "I am whatever I want to be. I am whatever I need to be." After receiving this assurance, Moses began making excuses.

> **Moses:** Why have You chosen me? I am not good at

speaking. I am slow in expressing myself; not only that, but I stutter when I speak.

Moses saw no comparison between Pharaoh and himself. He knew that the children of Israel were not going to believe him. God uses ordinary people, and Moses was one of those ordinary people. God solved Moses' excuses. He told Moses to take along his brother, Aaron, and let him do the talking. "Just tell him what to say after I tell you what to say."

Moses had no idea of what a mess he was going to encounter. It is good that God hides our future to spare our nerves! Several times Moses tried to convey the message from God to Pharaoh, but it was difficult to convince even the people he had been sent to rescue.

Not only did they not know Moses, but they also had no idea where they were going to live or what they would do. Moses was forewarned that Pharaoh would resist freeing the Israelites. Because of Pharaoh's refusal to let the people go, there was a series of plagues across Egypt, such as frogs and lice, flies and murrain, locusts, darkness and killing of the firstborn.

I cannot imagine what went through Moses' mind in the middle of this mess when he heard the people crying as death walked through the land. God made sure that death would pass over the Israelites by instructing them to sprinkle the blood of an unblemished lamb on the doorpost of their houses. After this tragic plague, Pharaoh reluctantly permitted the Israelites to leave. But Pharaoh was not ready to concede. After the people left, he sent his elite army to pursue, capture and re-enslave them.

Israelites: Moses! Look behind us! Pharoah's army is coming after us.
Moses: Yes, I see them.

THE MILEAGE, THE MESSAGE, AND THE MESS

Israelites: What are we going to do? The sea is in front of us; mountains are on both sides of us. Moses, we are trapped.

Moses: Don't worry. Just stand still and see what the Lord will do.

Israelites: Didn't we tell you to let us alone when you came to us about escaping? Didn't we tell you it would have been better for us to stay and serve the Egyptians rather than come out here to die?

Moses went to God on this matter. God said to him:

God: Moses, why are you standing here wasting your time crying to Me? Speak to the children and tell them to move on.

There is a time to pray and a time to act. Some of us spend more time begging than we do going forward with the promises of God. For example, if a man came to you hungry, is that the time to pray or to feed him? If a person came to you naked, would you pray for him or would you first find him some clothes?

God told Moses to stretch out his rod over the water, and when he obeyed, the water divided. All of the children of Israel crossed over on dry ground. Pharaoh's army followed in hot pursuit. When they were in the midst of the dry area, the waters came together and drowned every one of them. With all their doubts and skepticism, the Israelites realized that God was in control. We must not be too critical of them. They were people just as we are. They were subject to doubts and fears, just as we are. Far too often when we read the Bible, we think that people in those days were some kind of odd specimen. They were not. They were humans living in a world they could not understand and led by a God whom they could not see.

After crossing over and standing on the banks of the sea, they saw the work of God. As they stood there, they sang a victory song:

> He hath triumphed gloriously. The horse and the rider hath been thrown into the sea.
> The Lord is my strength and song, and he is become my salvation; he is my God, and I will prepare him an habitation, my father's God, and I will exalt him.
> Exodus 15:2

Three days after the crossing the people began murmuring again. They got on Moses' back, for they were without water to drink—out in the wilderness of Shur. The role of leader was never promised to be easy.

Israelites: Moses! We don't have any water to drink. The water in this well is not fit to drink. What are we going to do?

That was a legitimate gripe. They had to have water to drink, and the water they had found was not suitable. It was bitter. Moses again went to the Lord for help. The Lord instructed Moses to cut a tree branch and cast it into the water. Moses obeyed, and the water was made suitable to drink. The peace was not long-lasting. Coming into the wilderness of Sin, the people murmured against Moses and Aaron.

Israelites: I wish we could have died in Egypt where we could sit by the cooking pots and eat until we were full. Moses brought us out here to kill us.

They had become hungry and therefore, negative.

They were in a place where nothing would grow. Because it was so dry, the land was not suitable for planting. It must have been a very agonizing time for Moses. I often wonder how he managed to keep his sanity. The people did not realize that they were out there as an answer to their prayers. God had seen their plight down in Egypt, suffering and dying at the hands of the Egyptians. God sent Moses to lead them to freedom. Again may I say that those people were just as we are today. Far too often when God answers our prayers, we neither recognize nor are prepared to receive His answer. God will not be forced to respond to our needs and desires in the manner we wish.

God promised Moses that He would feed the Israelites bread from heaven: bread in the morning, flesh and manna in the evening.

After receiving strict instructions on how to gather the food, would you believe that some of the people did the opposite? Some people gathered so much food that they lost much of it to the worms. It is not hard for us to see that when we disobey God's direction, things go wrong. Moses' mess was getting messier; it was not over. After leaving the wilderness of Sin, the children of Israel came to the valley of Rephidim, and they found no water.

Israelites: Moses! There is no water. Give us water to drink.

Moses: Why are you nagging me about water? Why are you tempting God?

The people kept fussing and bickering.

Israelites: Moses! Why did you bring us out here to kill us, our children and our cattle?

Moses, as before, went to the Lord.

Moses: Lord, what must I do? These people are about to stone me.

Lord: Moses, I want you to take some of the elders of Israel and your rod, the same rod that you used at the Red Sea, and go to Horeb. With that rod, I want you to speak to a rock that I will show you so that the people will have water to drink.

Moses gathered the Israelites around the rock. But instead of speaking to the rock as he was commanded, he struck the rock twice in anger. Water came gushing out, and the people drank. However, this act would cost Moses dearly, and the mess continued as numerous problems occurred among the people. Moses tried to deal with all of the problems, but the pressure was wearing him down. His father-in-law, Jethro, recognized the dilemma.

As people stood in line with their complaints, Moses tried to deal with all this mess by himself.

Jethro: Moses, what are you doing? Why are you trying to deal with all this by yourself?

Moses: The people come to me to settle their differences. Whenever they come, I do what I've got to do. I try to get them to see and follow the will of God.

Jethro: What you are doing is no good; you are going to have a nervous breakdown dealing with all of this mess. You know you are not able to do all of this. Listen to me. Get some men you can depend on, and train them to deal with these little matters, and let the people bring the most serious problems to you.

Some of us are a little too proud to heed the advice of

others. It pays to listen. Moses did listen and selected some "class leaders." As pastors we must realize we cannot do everything, and there are people in our congregations who are much smarter than we. Yet, no matter what happens, we will get the blame and also the credit.

Moses was called by God to come up to Mount Sinai. There he communed with God for forty days and forty nights. God gave Moses the laws and ordinances by which the children of Israel were to live. While Moses was gone, the people doubted that Moses would come back. They did not know his whereabouts.

Israelites: Aaron, make us gods so that we may carry them ahead of us, because we don't know what has happened to Moses.

Aaron: All right, take off the golden earrings of your wives, your sons and your daughters, and bring them to me.

The people did what they were told, and Aaron melted down all that he had received and forged it into a golden calf. Not only that, he built an altar on which the calf sat. This was a mess. Out of all that the Lord had done for them, they still doubted and wanted a tangible god they could see and touch. They offered burnt offerings and peace offerings; they ate and drank. It is typical of many of us that after being blessed we forget the blessings of the Lord.

Lord: Moses, you better get back down to the people. They have become corrupt. They have completely forgotten what I have commanded them.

The Lord was vehemently angry, and wanted to destroy them all. Moses went down the mountain and came to the camp.

Moses: Aaron! What is going on here? What have you done?

Aaron: The people came to me and asked me to make them gods to go before them, because they thought you were not coming back. They thought you had abandoned them. I just wanted to please them.

Moses was so angry that he threw down the tablets and broke them. On the tablets were written the laws by which the children were to live.

Moses took the calf and ground it into dust then threw the residue in the waters. Moses took the blame for the people's action and interceded on their behalf. He went to God and asked to be punished for what they had done. God assured Moses that He would deal with those who had done the unthinkable. Moses was willing to give his life for the sins of his people. Some of us pastors often feel as Moses did. We want to take responsibility for the actions of our parishioners. We are only held responsible if we do not teach them the Lord's way. But if they hear and do not do the things which they ought, the blood will be on their hands.

Moses was getting old, and he called the people together and said, "I am a hundred and twenty years old this day. I can no more go out and come in; also the Lord hath said unto me, Thou shalt not go over this Jordan" (Deut. 31:1). Moses had blown his chance of entering the promised land because he had not followed God's instruction. As I stated before, Moses was told to speak to the rock, and the water would flow. But he was so disgusted he took his rod and struck the rock in fierce anger and said, "Come on, you rebels, and drink." God does not tolerate anyone mistreating His people, no matter how terrible they are. Listen to what God told Moses:

And the Lord said unto Moses, Behold, thou shalt sleep with thy fathers; and this people will rise up, and go a whoring after the gods of the strangers of the land, whither they go to be among them, and will forsake me, and break my covenant which I have made with them.
Then my anger shall be kindled against them in that day, and I will forsake them, and I will hide my face from them, and they shall be devoured, and many evils and troubles shall befall them, so that they will say in that day, are not these evils come upon us, because our God is not among us?
And I will surely hide my face in that day for all the evils which they shall have wrought, in that they are turned unto other gods. Deut. 31:16-18

I would think that perhaps Moses said to himself, "Did I go through all this for nothing? Was my work in vain?" I should say not. Moses brought the children of Israel out of slavery and within sight of the promised land. God never told Moses he would be successful. All Moses had to do was follow instructions. Many times we, as pastors, consider "throwing in the towel," but our commitment and dedication keep us going. Moses went up to the top of Mount Pisgah, where he viewed the promised land. God had told Moses why he would not be allowed to enter the land.

And the Lord spake unto Moses and Aaron, Because ye believed me not, to sanctify me in the eyes of the children of Israel, therefore ye shall not bring this congregation into the land which I have given them. Num. 20:12.

Moses gave his farewell message and admonished the people to follow God's commandments. Moses died and was buried in the land of Moab. Until this day no one knows where his grave is. From that day Moses was not seen by anyone. Matthew gives an account of the great meeting when Jesus took Peter, James and John up to a high mountain. While on that mountain something unusual happened. The face of Jesus shone bright as the sun, and His raiment became white as the light. And there appeared unto them Moses and Elias communing with Jesus. Wherever Moses was buried, today he is in the care of almighty God.

Blessed is the Nation whose God is the Lord, and the people whom he hath chosen for his own inheritance. Psalm 33:12

CHAPTER 3

Jonah Angry About God's Mercy

Nineveh, a city of approximately 120,000 people, had sunk to its lowest moral level. Robbery and murder were rampant, and the people cheated, lied and took advantage of one another. It was a bustling city, night and day. Everywhere, you could hear the cracking of whips, the prancing of horses and the rattling of chariots' wheels. People were lying in the street. Whoredom and witchcraft were prevalent. The Lord was furious and wanted to destroy the people. But before He did, He wanted to give them another opportunity to hear His warning words.

Enter a man named Jonah. God called Jonah and told him to get up and go to Nineveh and cry out against the city. Jonah did not want to go, so instead, he boarded a ship going in the opposite direction toward a city called Tarshish. Jonah knew about Nineveh's reputation and wanted no part of it. He did not want to get involved in their mess. After Jonah boarded a ship and went to sleep, the Lord sent a terrible storm and troubled the water. The sea became very turbulent. All that were aboard were afraid. They began throwing things overboard so that the ship would not sink.

The shipmaster found Jonah sleeping in the hull of the ship and woke him up. They wanted Jonah to pray to his God. "O sleeper, Arise and call upon thy God." If so be that God think upon us that we perish note often wonder why that statement was made, "Call upon thy God." Rather than call upon the Lord. Evidently these people were products of a polytheistic society.

They were not sure what was causing this turmoil, since it was not normal weather during that time of the year. Jonah finally confessed that he was the cause of the storm.

> **Men:** Tell us who is the cause of this turbulence.
> **Jonah:** I am a Hebrew, and it is I that fear the Lord.
> **Men:** Why did you do such a thing, putting our lives in jeopardy?
> **Jonah:** The Lord was sending me to Nineveh, to preach to those sinful people. And I don't want to go.
> **Men:** What must we do to you?
> **Jonah:** Just take me and throw me overboard.

The men tried hard to steer the ship to shore but were not successful. So, reluctantly, they threw Jonah into the sea. This was providence in action, for God had prepared a special fish just for this occasion. There have been many speculations about what kind of fish it was. Some say it could have been a whale; others say it could have been a shark. But whatever it was, it was especially prepared for Jonah. Jonah stayed in the belly of the fish for three days. Jonah prayed while in the fish's belly.

The Psalmist says it well:

> Whither shall I go from thy spirit? or whither shall I flee from thy presence? If I ascend up into heaven, thou art there; if I make my bed in hell, behold thou art there. If I take the wings of the morning and dwell in the uttermost parts of the sea; Even there shall thy hand lead me, and thy right hand shall hold me. Ps. 139:7-10

So you see, it didn't matter where Jonah went. He could not get out of the presence of God. On the third day the Lord caused the fish to vomit Jonah upon dry land. I am sure Jonah did not expect this to happen. God, as always, gave Jonah a second chance. He said to him, "Arise, go unto Nineveh, that great city, and preach unto it the preaching that I bid thee." So Jonah went, and the first day he arrived he predicted destruction of the people of Nineveh.

Jonah: You people better listen to me. You are going to be destroyed in forty days. You will be overthrown; just wait and see. The Lord said it and it is going to happen to every one of you.

After hearing this, the people were frightened and began to repent and fast. Even the king vacated his throne, took off his royal garb, covered himself with mourning cloth and sat in ashes. He sent out a decree that everyone, including the beasts, must fast and cover themselves in shame and repentance. They were heartily sorry for their wrongdoings. When God saw their needs, He decided not to punish them. In other words, God forgave them of their sins. God's change of plans made Jonah very angry, and he had the audacity to complain to the Lord.

Jonah: Lord! I knew You were going to do that. When I was in my own country, You told me to come here. That's why I ran away to Tarshish. I knew You were not going to do what You said. You are a merciful and gracious God. But now I'd rather be dead.

Jonah's problem was not that God had changed His mind. Jonah's problem was his ego. He was embarrassed because of all the things he had predicted, none had happened. Jonah's pride was at stake, not his mission. What Jonah didn't realize is that his mission was to preach to the people so that upon hearing the word, they might repent. If after hearing the word they did not repent, they would pay the consequences. Jonah expected for his prediction to be carried out and the mess eliminated. I'm sure that kind of thinking exists today. Some of us pastors would like to see some people punished. Some are waiting for certain of their foes to die, so that they may be able to have a productive ministry. But what we don't realize is that when those die, there will be others.

We should never expect to have a congregation of people who never oppose us. Those people keep us humble. Jonah, in his anger, went outside the city and made himself some kind of shelter and sat under it. Then he waited to see what the Lord was going to do to the people of Nineveh. His shelter was made out of leaves. When the sun came up, the leaves withered. In order to teach Jonah a lesson on compassion, God allowed a large plant to grow over Jonah's head to keep him from the scorching sun. When morning came God sent a worm to destroy that very plant which He had prepared. It is a true saying: "The Lord giveth and the Lord taketh away." Jonah had more compassion on the plant than he had for the people of Nineveh. In the midst of this ordeal, Jonah wanted to die rather than endure the heat.

We are troubled on every side, yet not distressed; we are perplexed, but not in despair; Persecuted, but not forsaken; cast down but not destroyed. 2 Corinthians 4:8-9

CHAPTER 4

God's Odd Couple

Ihave known one man in my life who knowingly married a prostitute. He met her while out on the town. He fell in love with her and proposed marriage. She accepted. As far as I know, today they are still married and are living happy and productive lives. It is not an easy thing to admit that your wife is a former prostitute. But we must keep in mind that there are qualities in each of us, regardless of what we are and do, that are worth salvaging.

The Bible tells of a prophet named Hosea, who was given a directive by God to go take a wife of whoredom. Not only was he to marry her, but she would be unfaithful to him and have children while in her whorish practice. God had a message to convey, and Hosea was in for a terrible mess. Hosea's children were to be living messages to the people. Permit me at this point to say that "whoredom" is not restricted only to sexual promiscuity.

Whenever we speak of adultery, we automatically think about sexuality. But whenever we commit ourselves to God and then go and serve other gods, we commit adultery. We may point the finger of scorn at people we see on street corners, but there are some of us who worship things that become our gods, and that is just as dangerous as those who are on the streets.

I cannot imagine what was in Hosea's mind when he was told to marry a whore. I wonder what people would say today if they heard their pastor was down on the strip looking for a wife. I also wonder what the people in Hosea's time said about his marrying a prostitute. It must have been a difficult thing to do.

This was some mess, and it would be messier today for many of us. In spite of that, Hosea did as he was directed, and that is the main focus—obedience. Hosea married Gomer.

Gomer had three children, and each of them was to be a message to the people. Jezreal was the name of the first, which meant, "For yet a little while and I will avenge the blood of Jezreal." Loruhamah was the name of the second, which meant, "I will no longer have mercy upon the house of Israel.". Loammi, a second son, was meant to convey that "For ye are not my people, and I will not be your God." Each of the children, two sons and a daughter, was a message.

Gomer did not stop her indiscriminate mingling. She went back to her lovers. Her suitors took care of her by giving her bread, water, wool, flax, oil and other things.

Hosea thought he would ask the children for help in changing Gomer's ways. He pleaded with them to plead with their mother.

Hosea: Ammi! Ruhamah! Go talk to your mother and plead with her to stop her whoring around. If she doesn't I will strip her naked down to her bare bottom. I will not give her nay to drink so that she may thirst. I will make life hard for her. She will go looking for her lovers and will not find them. I will make life miserable for her until she returns to me.

God: Hosea! Go get your wife, no matter what it costs. Go get her and love her, even though she loves what she is doing. Get her and bring her back.

Hosea obeyed the Lord and bought Gomer back for fifteen dollars and eight bushels of barley.

Hosea: Gomer! I want you to live alone for a few days, and I don't want you to see anybody. You are not to play around on me anymore. You are not to see any man. You are going to be mine, only mine.

God put Hosea through this terrible mess to get a message to the house of Israel. They had left their first love and gone whoring after other gods. No matter how wayward we may be, God still loves us and summons us to return. God still blesses us, but we take His blessings and serve other gods. Not only that but we give that which is holy to the dogs. These people had completely forgotten God. They were swearing, stealing and committing adultery and violence in the streets. But in spite of all that, God waited for the return of his children.

No wonder the hymn-writer penned it so well: "How great the wisdom, power and grace which in redemption shine." Hosea had his exposure to the mileage, the message and the mess.

Beloved, think it not strange concerning the
fiery trial which is to try you, as though some
strange thing happened unto you. Peter 4:12

Tears of Jeremiah

Oh that my head were waters, and mine eyes a fountain of tears, that I might weep day and night for the slain of the daughter of my people. Jer. 9:1

Those are the words of Jeremiah, who came to be known as the weeping prophet. He had been called by God to be a prophet.

God: Jeremiah! Before you were conceived in the belly of your mother I knew you, and before you were born I ordained you to be a prophet unto the nations.

Jeremiah: Lord! You know that I can't speak, and I am only a child.

God: Jeremiah! Don't tell me you are a child. You will go wherever I send you, and whatever I tell you to say you will say it. Don't be afraid of their facial expressions, for I will be with you.

Jeremiah, just as Moses, found some logical reasons for not wanting to be chosen for the task God had set. I want to digress here to express my sincere argument against abortion, for here we see clearly that even before Jeremiah was conceived, God knew him and ordained him for a work. Those who claim that there is no life in the womb and no personality, are treading on the dangerous ground of murder. We don't know who we are killing by permitting people to murder unborn children. This is dangerous business.

God told Jeremiah, "You will go where I send you and say what I tell you." Here we see the mileage and the message, and when God said, "Don't let their faces frighten you," Jeremiah knew there was going to be a mess. Jeremiah's mouth was touched by God. He was to root out and pull down and destroy in order to build and to plant. What a tremendous task for such a young lad. We must recognize that responsibility knows no age. Jeremiah, by now, knew what he was in for. The people would be mean-looking and hostile, but God had prepared Jeremiah for those arrogant, hostile people. We must not forget that these were people who practiced the worship of many gods. Each family had its own gods: gods of wood and gods of stone. They gave reverence to the wooden god as their father and to the stone god as their mother. Jeremiah had a difficult task before him. But we know that nothing is too hard for the Lord.

Jeremiah was told, "Go cry in the ears of Jerusalem." These people whom God had delivered and blessed were guilty of apostasy; they had gone after other gods. God had a message to give Jeremiah for the people to hear and understand. God sent Jeremiah down to a potter's house. He wanted Jeremiah to watch what the potter was doing because what he saw would be a message. Jeremiah saw the potter take a flawed vessel and put it back on the wheel and fashion it and remold it until the flaws were smoothed out. God said to Jeremiah, "I can do to these people what the potter has done to the vessel." No wonder we sing:

Have thine own way Lord, have Thine own
way; Thou art the potter, I am the clay. Mold me
and make me after Thy will, while I am waiting
yielded and still.

No matter how bad we are, no matter how rotten we
are, none of us is so bad that God cannot change us.

Jeremiah was about twenty-one years old when he was
given this awesome task. He had to cry judgement upon his
people, no matter how painful it was. His prophecy was not
accepted. Let us look at a litany of "mess" that Jeremiah
endured:

Jehoiakim tried to silence him; the people plotted to
kill him. He was accused of treason and thrown into a
dungeon of slime, regarded as meddler and traitor and not
permitted to marry.

Jeremiah was under a "divine imperative." He was
devoted to God. After forty years of prophesying, some
believe he was stoned to death. Other writers think he died
of old age.

Jeremiah was known as the prophet with a broken
heart. Regardless of how he died, we can see clearly the
mileage, the message and the mess.

For I am come to set a man at variance against
his father, and the daughter against her mother,
and the daughter-in-law against her mother-in-
law. Matthew 10:35

CHAPTER 6

A Moving Testimony

In the year King Uzziah died, I saw the Lord sitting upon a throne, high and lifted up, and his train filled the temple. Isaiah 6:1

This scripture is a moving testimony of a man named Isaiah. Isaiah was related to King Uzziah, who died of leprosy. Uzziah was made king in his early teens, and he ruled for fifty-two years. He was successful in all his undertakings. He did that which was right in the sight of the Lord. He built towers, dug wells, put together great fighting armies and won many battles. Many new inventions were made during his reign. Uzziah, like many of us today, got on an ego trip and transgressed against the Lord. He was well known all over the country. Uzziah did well as long as he performed within his jurisdiction. But one day he overstepped his authority. He went into the temple and tried to take over the duties that were delegated to consecrated priests. He went into the temple to light the candlesticks and carried in his hand the censer on which was the fire/light. When the priest confronted him, he became beligerent. While he held the censer, leprosy broke out on his forehead. He became gravely ill and never recovered.

After being moved from place to place, he finally died. There is a lesson for all of us to learn. We should never undertake the performance of duties that we are not qualified to do or are not consecrated to execute. Thus came the words at the beginning of this chapter: "In the year King Uzziah died, I saw the Lord."

Isaiah, being related to the king, had the run of the temple. He may have gone into the temple to pray or mourn. But during that visit, he had a vision. It is this writer's opinion that King Uzziah was admired by Isaiah and that he stood somewhat in the way of Isaiah's calling.

He was the central figure in Isaiah's life. In that vision Isaiah saw celestial beings called seraphim standing before the throne of the Lord. The term *seraphim* means "burying ones." Just as God got the attention of Moses through the burning bush, he got the attention of Isaiah through the "flaming angels." There is no record of how many there were, but each of them had six wings. Two wings covered their face, two wings covered their feet and the other two were used to fly. Isaiah heard them cry to one another, "Holy, holy, holy is the Lord of hosts; the whole earth is full of His glory." (Is. 6:3). Something was happening to Isaiah on the inside. I am not speaking of the inside of the temple, but on the inside of the man. Isaiah was shaken by the smoke that filled the temple. He was so shaken that he verbally expressed his sinful condition.

> Woe is me! for I am undone, because I am a man
> of unclean lips, and I dwell in the midst of a
> people of unclean lips; for mine eyes have seen
> the King, the Lord of hosts.

Isaiah admitted that he had a foul mouth and was living amongst a people of the same condition. He admitted that he was not worthy of experiencing such glory. It is only when we have been dealt with on the inside that we confess with our lips. Isaiah saw his fault and admitted his guilt. He was experiencing the process of cleansing. One of the seraphim flew down with a "live" coal in his hand. With tongs, he took the coal off the altar and placed it upon Isaiah's mouth. That process took away Isaiah's inquiry and purged his sin.

After being cleansed, Isaiah heard the voice of God.

Lord: Whom shall I send, and who will go for us?

The answer was not suprising. After being purged of his sin and experiencing the glory of God, the response was obvious.

Isaiah: Here I am, send me.

We must keep in mind the title of this book, *The Mileage, The Message and The Mess.*

Lord: Isaiah! Go tell the people they hear but don't understand, they see but don't know what they see.
Isaiah: How long will it be before they are ready to listen?
Lord: Not until their cities are destroyed, without a person left, and the whole country is an utter wasteland, and they are all taken away as slaves to other countries far away.

God was angry at the people for their disobedience. He expressed this anger in the following words:

> Hear, O heaven, and give ear, O earth, for the
> Lord hath spoken, I have nourished and brought
> up children, and they have rebelled against me.
> The ox knoweth his owner and the ass his
> master's crib; but Israel doth not know, my
> people doth not consider. Is. 1:2-3

Isaiah had a mess on his hands. The children he saw were sick, weak and faint. From head to feet they were covered with bruises and welts and infected wounds, unanointed and unbound. These graphic descriptions of the conditions of the people were presented through allegories. God was fed up with their burnt sacrifices and blood of slain rams and other animals. Their celebrations were in vain. All of the sacrifices they made could not erase their sins. These were the people to whom Isaiah was to prophesy.

Let us listen to their "woes":

> Woe! unto the wicked; it shall be ill with him for the
> reward of his hands shall be given him.
> Woe! unto them that join house to house, that lay field
> to field, till there be no place, that they may be placed
> alone in the midst of the earth.
> Woe! unto them that rise up early in the morning, that
> they may follow strong drink; that continue until
> night, till wine inflame them!
> Woe! unto them that draw iniquity with cords of vanity,
> and sin as it were with a cart rope.
> Woe! unto them that call evil good, and good evil; that
> put darkness for light, and light for darkness; that put
> bitter for sweet and sweet for bitter.
> Woe! unto them that are mighty to drink wine, and men
> of strength to mingle strong drink.
> Woe! unto them that are wise in their own eyes, and
> prudent in their own sight.

People are the same today as they were in yesteryears. They did not listen to the prophets before Isaiah, and they did not listen to him nor those who followed. It is not certain how Isaiah died, but it is assumed that he died of old age.

> Blessed are ye, when men shall revile you, and persecute you, and shall say all manner of evil against you falsely, for my sake.
> Rejoice, and be exceeding glad; for great is your reward in heaven; for so persecuted they the prophets which were before you. Matthew 5:11-12

CHAPTER 7

Saul Spiritually Arrested

During the days of the early church, there was a man named Saul who thought Christians were heretics and therefore, enemies of Jehovah, worthy of death. He secured orders to arrest anyone found calling on the name Jesus. This is the same man who made mockery of the church, and who stood and held the coats of those who stoned Stephen to death. Saul was a devout Jew and was well trained in Jewish history and doctrines. While on the way to Damascus to punish Christians in that city, he was struck with blindness by a bright light as he fell to the ground. He was asked but one question:

Jesus: Saul, Saul, why persecutest thou me?
Saul: Who art thou, Lord?
Jesus: I am Jesus whom thou persecutest.

Let us take note here how Saul responded to his name. He did not say, "Who is that calling my name?" He said, "Who are you, Lord?" In other words, he knew who it was. To use our terms: "Is that you, Lord?" There were others traveling with him who heard the voice, but they saw no one.

Saul was afraid, for he had come face to face with the one he had been persecuting. Trembling, he asked the question:

Saul: What wilt thou have me to do?
Jesus: Arise, and go into the city, and it shall be told thee what thou must do.

One thing we must quickly recognize is that Saul was dedicated to what he believed. Jesus did not turn Saul back but told him to go on to where he was going. There lived a man in Damascus named Ananias who was given the task of informing Saul of what he was called to do.

Jesus: Ananias! There is a man called Saul of Tarsus waiting for you. He had a vision of you coming to put your hand on him so that he may receive his sight.
Ananias: Lord! I have heard about this man. He is evil, a murderer, and I don't want anything to do with him.

It is a truth that our reputation travels much faster than we imagine. Jesus told Ananias not to worry about Saul, because now he was on God's side.

Jesus: Ananias! I have chosen him as a vessel to bridge the gap and spread My name to the gentiles.

How ironic it is, that Saul was sent to a place on "Straight" street. Whenever Jesus has anything to do with us, we are put on "straight" street. Reluctantly Ananias went and found Saul.

Ananias: Brother Saul, the Lord who appeared unto you in the way as thou camest hath sent me, that thou mightest receive thy sight, and be filled with the Holy Ghost.

As soon as Ananias laid hands on Saul, something fell from his eyes like scales, and he regained his sight. It is noteworthy that whenever the Holy Ghost takes control of our lives, the scales of confusion, hatred, anger, misunderstanding and narrow-mindness fall from our "eyes." We see clearly when we receive the power and presence of the Holy Ghost.

I am certain that Saul had no idea what was in store for him, even after all of the evil he had done. He did not realize that after accepting the call to go, he would be in for a lot of mess. The first sign of trouble Saul had was after he began to preach in the synagogue. People could not believe what they heard. They could not accept easily the idea that this man, who had been a murderer, could now be preaching Christ.

It is typical even today for us to be skeptical of the people we once knew as drunkards, addicts and criminals. The skepticism comes because we know people use conversion as a front to continue what they were previously doing. However, Saul, in spite of suspicion and skepticism, kept preaching about Christ and His crucifixion. The Jews saw that Saul had betrayed them and so plotted to kill him. This man Saul, who had stood by while Stephen was stoned, this man who took it upon himself to imprison and persecute those who called upon the name Jesus, now found his life in jeopardy. After receiving information about a threat on his life, some of the disciples had to lower him over the wall of the city in a basket to get him away to safety. Even after fleeing to Jerusalem, the disciples there were afraid of him. Barnabas had to convince the others that Saul was a changed man, truly converted and therefore one of them. Since Christ came to save the world, Saul was used as the vehicle which gave the gentiles equal opportunity to salvation. Through his conversion Saul saw the error in his blatant activity against the followers of Christ. He had a message to carry to the gentiles, but I am sure he had no idea of the mess he would encounter. Soon after accepting the call, Saul had to put in the mileage, endure the mess and deliver the message of a living Savior. Saul later came to be called Paul and continued his mission. Without further delay, let us look at the litany of Paul's mess.

Litany
Paul had to flee for his life from the Jews (Acts 9:23-25).

The disciples at Jerusalem were afraid of him (Acts 9:26-29).

A serious division arose between Paul and Barnabas (Acts 15:36-41).

Paul and Silas were beaten, stripped of their clothing and put into prison (Acts 16:19-24).

After hearing that Paul was preaching in Berea, some Jews from Thessalonica came there and stirred up the people against him (Acts 17:11-14).

Paul received assurance from a vision (Acts 18:9-11).

Paul had to change his itinerary while in Greece; he was going to sail to Syria but changed his route to call on Macedonia (Acts 19:1-3).

Paul set out for the temple and found himself in the hands of a mob (Acts 21:27-31).

Paul was rescued by a captain, bound by two chains and

required to show some kind of identification (Acts 21:31-40).

Paul defended himself (Acts 22).

A band of Jews swore not to eat until Paul was killed (Acts 23:12-14).

Paul avoided an ambush through the knowledge of his sister's son (Acts 23:16-26).

Paul was accused of being a pestilent fellow and a supporter of sedition (Acts 24:1-9).

Paul had to defend himself to Felix (Acts 24).

Paul defended himself before King Agrippa and told of his conversion (Acts 26).

En route to Italy, Paul's warning was ignored concerning the condition of the ship on which they were sailing (Acts 27).

A shipwreck caused sheer panic. God assured Paul of their safety (Acts 27).

Paul was bitten by a viper on the island of Melita (Acts 28:3-6).

Paul tried to explain his situation to the chief of the Jews but to no avail (Acts 28:17-31).

Paul was confined to a cold, damp dungeon and deserted by Demas. He requested that Timothy bring his cloak and parchment that he had left at Carpus' house (2 Tim. 4:10-13).

For the sake of the Lord Jesus Christ, here Paul sat. Nearing his impending death and shivering in a damp cell, he continued to hold on to the faith.

Let us listen to what he had to say concerning his experiences:

> But none of these things move me, neither count
> I my life dear unto myself, so that I might finish
> my course with joy, and the ministry which I

have received of the Lord Jesus, to testify the gospel of the grace of God. (Acts 20:24).

In spite of what happened to Paul, he held his commitment. The dedicated person who was close to destroying the church, was transformed and dedicated to spreading the gospel of the church. There are two different accounts of how Paul died. It is recorded that Paul was beheaded on the Ostian Way. The other account is that he was beheaded in Rome by Emperor Nero. But whatever the record shows, we could never deny the mileage, the message and the mess that Paul endured.

Fear none of those things which thou shalt suffer; behold that the devil shall cast some of you into prison that ye may be tried; and ye shall have tribulation ten days; be thou faithful unto death, and I will give thee a crown of life. Revelation 2:20

CHAPTER 8

Only Faithfulness is Required

Having been a student of the Bible for many years, I have carefully searched the Scriptures and never found one prophet, judge, teacher or disciple who died believing he was successful in his work for the Lord. Not one died satisfied that he had accomplished what he set out to do. God never told them, nor is he telling us, to be successful.

All God requires of us is our faithfulness. I see life as a relay race. There are starters, there are middle runners and there are those who carry the baton to the finish line. The starters carry the baton to the next runners. They hand the baton to the other runners and say to them, "You take it from here." In this race we run and carry the baton of spiritual morality and faithfulness to other people and say to them, "Pass it on." Sometimes through neglect, ignorance, compromises and a desire to fulfill personal ambition some of us drop the baton. But God always has someone waiting to pick up the baton and say to Him, "Lord, I will take it from here."

Some of us may have a more difficult time than others, but one thing is for sure: the race must continue. Adam and Eve were given the baton first, but through their disobedience they dropped the baton. But God had Noah waiting to pick it up, and from there he brought it to this side of the flood. From Noah down through the ages God has had runners: runners who ran into a lot of "mess," runners who sometimes lost hope, and runners who did not think they were worthy to be chosen. There is one thing worth remembering, and that is: God always calls ordinary people. Whenever God had a task to be performed, he never selected military leaders; He never called men who were not doing anything. They all were busy doing something. Moses was busy tending his flock; David was tending sheep; Elisha was busy plowing with twelve yoke of oxen; Gideon was busy threshing wheat; Matthew was busy collecting taxes; Peter and Andrew were busy fishing; James and his brothers were mending their nets. Others were also deeply involved in their professions.We must carefully consider our true calling before we commit ourselves to the call.

> For which of you, intending to build a tower, sitteth not down first, and counteth the cost, whether he have sufficient to finish it. Luke 14:28

Do you have what it takes to run your leg of the race? Are you willing to endure the mess, the pain of rejection and scorn? No one told us that the road would be easy. People today are no different from those of history. The prophets dealt with stiff-necked and impudent people.

THE MILEAGE, THE MESSAGE, AND THE MESS

Today there is nothing new. We must not become weary, and we must not become faint.

> But they that wait upon the Lord shall renew
> their strength; they shall mount up with wings
> as eagles; they shall run and not be weary, and
> they shall walk and not faint. Is. 40:31

There are two things that we must never do: 1) attempt to defend God, and 2) try to understand God. God is God all by Himself. All the things we do, we do through faith. Faithfulness is the key to service.

Let us take a look at some who made the choice to follow Jesus:

John the Baptist was beheaded.

Stephen was stoned to death.

Matthew was slain with a sword somewhere in Ethiopia.

Mark died after being dragged through the streets of Alexandria.

Luke was hanged upon an olive tree in Greece.

John was put into a caldron of boiling oil. He escaped and then was banished to the Isle of Patmos.

James the Greater was beheaded at Jerusalem.

James the Lesser was thrown from a pinnacle of the temple and then beaten to death.

Bartholomew was skinned alive and died.

Andrew was bound to a cross and died while he was yet preaching.

Thomas had a lance driven through his body in East India.

Jude was shot to death with arrows.

Matthias was stoned and then beheaded.

Paul was beheaded at Rome by Emperor Nero.

> I reckon that the sufferings of this present time
> are not worthy to be compared with the glory
> which shall be revealed in us. Rom. 8:18

What Paul was saying is, the mess that he underwent was nothing when compared with the reward Jesus will make known to us and through us. There is a song that says, "No one told me that the road would be easy, I don't believe he brought me this far to leave me." This song captures what Paul was expressing. When we commit ourselves completely to the work of the Lord, no mess is messy enough to turn us around.

There is a reward for those who remain faithful to the calling. There are countless others unknown to the world, but surely known to God, who have been slain because they held up the name of Jesus. Some Christians were thrown in the lions' den just for the sport of it. Others were denied the right of religious expression, just for the sake of Christ. While John was in exile on the Isle of Patmos, he had a revelation from Jesus Christ. He saw the past, the present and the future. John saw the Lamb open the fifth seal. There he saw under the altar the souls of those who had been slain for the Word of God and the testimony which they held. Voices cried out, "How long will it be before our murderers and tormentors are brought to justice and our blood defended by them on earth?" And the answer came with a profound: "Until your fellow servants also and their brethren, that should be killed as they were, should be fulfilled." To put it plainly, there are those of us who must also undergo the same kind of "mess" as those souls under the altar.

"Shall I be carried to the sky on flowery beds of ease while others fought to win the prize and sailed through bloody seas? Are there no foes for me to face? Must I not stem the flood? Is this ole world a friend to grace to help me on to God?"

Sure I must fight if I would win. Increase my courage, Lord. I bear the toil endure the pain, supported by thy Word.

John also saw 144,000 and then looked and saw a number that no man could number. And the question came, "Who are they?" These are they who have washed their robes (undergone the mess) in the blood of the lamb.

If we have a thorough belief in our divine calling, and let our words and our actions be inspired by God, we will pass on from victory to victory. We will rise step by step, using the messes that we encounter as plateaus toward higher heights. And when we reach the top, our ever-broadening outlook will reveal to us the incomparable beauty and purpose of our service as messengers of Christ.

> But beware of men: for they will deliver you up
> to the councils, and they will scourge you in
> their synagogues. Matthew 10:17

CHAPTER 9

Don't Ever Laugh at God

There is a time to laugh. But never is there a time to laugh at God. We laugh for joy, and we laugh for derision—which means ridicule or scorn. Laughter is very much a part of humankind. It is one of the things that distinguishes us from animals. Of all of the species of living organisms, mankind is the only one that has the privilege and capacity to laugh. We laugh at other people; we laugh at ourselves. Some of us laugh on the outside, but at the same time we are crying on the inside. Some of us don't know when to laugh. There is a time to weep and a time to laugh. But never is there a time to laugh at God.

Laughter is not only an expression of the face or the exposing of one's teeth. Laughter can be the arrogance of the heart and defiance of the soul. Laughter is also an attitude.

When God informed Abraham that his wife, Sarah, was

going to become a mother, Abraham fell to the ground laughing hysterically. In his heart he pondered, Shall a child be born unto him that is one hundred years old? Not only that, but Sarah was long past her child-bearing age. She was ninety years old. Abraham was looking at the impossibility of Sarah becoming pregnant. We get ourselves in a mess when we attempt to ridicule God. For we know that nothing is impossible for God. God sent three men to verify that Sarah was going to have a child. Sarah, in the other room, heard this, and she laughed within her heart. God questioned Abraham concerning Sarah. We have to assume that Abraham confronted Sarah. Sarah denied that she laughed. There are times when we may outwardly deny what we do, but we can never deny our action before God. God knows what we do even before we do it. The question is asked: Is anything too hard for the Lord?

When Nehemiah learned the condition of the people that were left in Jerusalem from the captivity, he was sorry and wanted to do something about rebuilding the city. There were two men named Sanballat and Tobiah who did not like the idea and were bent on putting a stop to the undertaking. Because God was on Nehemiah's side, the work was started, but these two men, Sanballat and Tobiah, laughed Nehemiah to scorn. They thought it was an insult to the king.

These men were not only laughing at Nehemiah, they were laughing at God. It is a terrible thing when we don't know what or whom we are laughing at. In spite of the opposition, the wall was rebuilt, and those who laughed were not laughing anymore. The wall was built because the people had a mind to work. Sanballat and Tobiah set out to put a stop to the rebuilding. But through prayer and dedication, the Israelites were able to finish their weapons, and they were able to finish the wall. Some of us never know when to quit opposing God's work. One thing is for sure, nobody can obstruct the work of the Lord.

Out there on the battlefield, David saw the trouble that his people were in, and he offered himself to go fight the giant Goliath. After putting on the armor, David found it cumbersome, and took off the fighting equipment. Instead, he took a sling and five pebbles and went to meet this giant. When Goliath saw David—young, small and ill-trained— he laughed. But we all know that his laughing cost him his head. Goliath didn't know that he was laughing, not at David, but at the Lord. But the laughter was soon wiped from his face.

Many of us don't realize that we too in our own ways laugh at God. It was the writer James who wrote: "Let your laughter be turned into mourning." Sorrow is better than laughter. We too laugh at God, in many ways, in our heart. We laugh at God when we receive His blessings and never give thanks, and when we fail to show any remorse for our wrongdoings. We laugh at God when we verbally declare Him to be first in our life, but in actuality put him last on our agenda. We laugh at God when we praise Him with our tongue and with the same tongue curse His creation. We must keep in mind that man's complexity is God's simplest task.

When Jesus was nailed to the cross, the Jews pointed their fingers and laughed because Jesus had declared that He was the Son of God, but He would not make an attempt to save Himself. But the believers know that early on Sunday morning, the laughter turned into fear for some and joy for others. We should never laugh at God.

Chapter 10

Mess Holds Us in Check

We must keep in mind that trouble (mess) is not a finality. The mess that we may encounter can be either a friend or a foe. There are hidden advantages/opportunities whenever we are confronted with trouble. Mess leaves its imprint upon our personality and our character. When mess comes it brings with it lessons for us to learn. It teaches us humility, patience, understanding and self-control. Far too often we become anxious to strike back at the mess, and we inadvertently botch it up worse than it would have been if we had left it alone. If you fan a fire, the flames will grow larger.

Mess gives us a wake-up call. If we, as leaders, never had any kind of trouble, we would become rambunctious children whom God would have to discipline again and again. Just look at what happened to King Nebuchadnezzar. One morning he walked out in the palace garden and said, "Is this not the great Babylon, that I have built for the house of the kingdom by the might of my power, and for the honor of my majesty?" And before he finished making this arrogant speech, God took his kingdom away. He became as a wild man. So if we had everything like we wanted it all the time, we too would become rambunctious.

When we reflect on the mess that the prophets, the judges and the disciples endured, compared to the mess we are undergoing, we could easily say that our mess is minor. No matter how bad we may think things are, no matter how hopeless things may seem, we must remind ourselves that "it came to pass."

It was Paul who wrote to the Corinthians, "Therefore I take pleasure in infirmities, in reproaches, in necessities, in persecutions, in distresses for Christ's sake; for when I am weak, then I am strong" (2 Cor. 12:10). We are also to be reminded that "weeping may endure for a night, but joy cometh in the morning" (Ps. 30:5).

> For our light affliction, which is but for a moment, worketh for us a far more exceeding and eternal weight of glory. 2 Corinthians 4:17

Contemporary Mess

I interviewed various pastors to see what kind of messes they are now undergoing. Some of these will not surprise you. Some I can identify with, but none, as I stated earlier, can be compared with those of the past.

A. Persons are angry because their pastor did/does not address them by their academic title.

My Opinion: In the house of the Lord, we accept each other as brother and sister. Those who desire or demand to be called by their academic title in church are insecure or just on an ego trip. I would have no reservations in addressing those persons by their title if I went to see them at their work place or any other place.

B. People who wanted the pastor to move away because they could not stand his wife.

My Opinion: There are many underlying reasons for women not to like each other. Members must keep in mind that the pastor was assigned to that charge, and with him comes his wife. I must hastily admit that I have seen pastors' wives overstep their boundaries. And that is because the power was given to them by their husbands. If the women are concerned about the attitude of the pastor's wife or husband, there is a Christian approach that they may take to help curtail this problem. We must also keep in mind that some members will never be satisfied.

C. Facing stiff opposition from a few who did not want to rebuild.

My Opinion: We must acknowledge first that no matter what project we may undertake, we will never get one hundred percent participation. The mistake some of us preachers make is, unless we get the approval of certain influential members in our congregation, we feel that we will fail. We have made the grave mistake of empowering certain members who we believe are financially secure. To those preachers I have this to say: "If God be for us, who will be against us?" If we go about securing approval of the congregation as prescribed, there should be no doubt about the outcome.

D. Members of the church insist on knowing where every penny is spent before they give any more money.

My Opinion: Those persons who are always insisting on knowing where each dime is spent are those who never attend a city council meeting, never attend a county meeting and never attend a school board meeting. The government wastes more of our tax dollars than any other organization. The church is not a savings and loan company, nor is it a bank. When you give your money to the church, it is no longer yours. How is it that people raise so much fuss over the money they give the local church, and they send dollars upon dollars to some television minister they don't know and will never know? When a member becomes ill, or when one of their children gets into trouble, they don't call the television minister. They go to the pastor of their local church.

E. Certain people in the church cannot/will not work together.

My Opinion: The church is a group of "baptized believers." We become a family. We must admit that there will always be some differences because we are different. Each first Sunday when we extend the call to the Lord's supper, we say, "Ye that do truly and earnestly repent of your sins, and are in love and charity with your neighbor etc." We come flocking to the front to partake of this great meal still harboring animosity in our hearts. There may be many underlying reasons why people cannot work together. And many times it is very personal. Some, we as pastors, cannot deal with. If we tried to deal with something we know nothing about, we would create a fury that would never subside. The individuals involved must put forth efforts to solve their differences.

F. Members are always angry and complaining about something.

My Opinion: Some of us are always puffed up about something. Some are angry because they don't get any personal attention. Some folks like to be courted and petted. Some are angry, not necessarily at the preacher, but because something is not right in their lives. They may have a sorry husband/wife and cannot or will not talk about their pain. Jealousy is sometimes the main factor. Folks get angry if they don't see their name in the church bulletin. Or because they are not made chairperson over a certain commission. There is an approach that each of us can take. That is to try to make life pleasant for others, say something good about them, and let them know that we recognize their presence. It is frustrating to see people with "rocks" in their jaws and not know what they are angry about. There is a song I remember that goes like this:

"When you're smiling, when you're smiling, the whole world smiles with you. When you're laughing, the sun comes shining through."

We can rest assured that if there is any trouble in our congregation, it is caused by church members. Unchurched folk never bother churches. So what kind of signal are we sending when we have to spend money in civil court and sue one another for things that should be settled in our meetings through proper procedures? The church will always have trouble (mess) because we cannot assume that all members in our congregation are converted and committed. The shoe fits on both feet. If we continue putting in the mileage, and carrying the message, then we will surely encounter some mess.

> I reckon that the sufferings of this present time
> are not worthy to be compared with the glory
> which shall be revealed in us. Romans 8:18

CHAPTER 12

Human Wrecks

All of us are familiar with wrecks. Either we have seen wrecks or we have been involved in them. Wrecks are prevalent in our society. We hear about planes crashing, shipwrecks, train wrecks and automobile wrecks constantly. When there is a wreck, and the collision is so bad that the driver can't move the vehicle, a tow truck must be called. Most of the time the driver of the tow truck does not repair the vehicle. What he does is pull the vehicle into the shop so that the expert repairman may work to restore it. Sometimes a vehicle is too damaged to repair, so it is considered a total loss and sent on to a junkyard. I have seen junkyards with autos stacked in piles after piles; they are there because they are beyond repair and have been declared "totalled."

Most of us know about wrecks, but many of us are not aware that there are human wrecks. The horror of human wrecks is far beyond anything that we may describe. You may look in any city, on any street, or in any alley, and you will see human wrecks. You may see physical damages as a result of moral collisions. There will also be broken spirits that cause people to become social outcasts.

We see the results of broken homes, broken hearts, broken spirits, shattered dreams, deranged personalities, warped characters and unstable minds. These are wrecks on the highway of life. What are we to do? Must we pass them by?

Some wrecked auto may need only dents knocked out; others need welding, and some may need to be painted. Still others need new parts and so forth. Human wrecks need the same attention and repair that autos get. But someone must tow them in to the place of repair. We do know that no human can be classed as "totalled." The church is the place for repair, and we ministers and laymen alike are tow trucks. We need to hook up to those wrecks and pull them in.

God does not have a junkyard on which to place human wrecks. That is the reason why God sent Jeremiah down to the potter's house. The potter worked on the damaged pottery until all the flaws were gone. Those that were beyond repair were thrown out in the potter's field. Jeremiah saw the message and at that point knew he had to become a towtruck for God.

Large vehicles need larger tow trucks. So we can't assume we are going to be able to tow all of the wrecks with the same truck. The tow truck that we send must be able to pull in the wreck. We may even turn the wreck into a worse wreck if we are not careful how we pull them in.

Jesus saw a human wreck up in the Gadarenes, pulled him in, repaired his character, smoothed out the kinks, straightened out his tongue and restored his right mind. Jesus had no intentions of placing this man in a junkyard.

Four human tow trucks brought a human wreck to the repairman, Jesus, in the story of the man on a stretcher who was sick with palsy. His friends even tore up a roof to get this physical wreck into the presence of Jesus.

And he was repaired.

There is a great need for more tow trucks for Christ. The church is the repair shop and Jesus is the repairman.

When Jesus said, "Go ye onto the highways and into the hedges and compel men to come," He sent us out as tow trucks to pull in the wrecks. The Samaritan on the Jericho road was a tow truck when he saw a man who had fallen among thieves and was left for dead. The Samaritan picked him up, put him on his beast and brought him into town so that he could be treated. Unlike the priest and the Levite, this unknown man used his tow truck to help somebody he didn't know, because he knew Somebody. Let us keep in mind, no matter how messy the wreck is, tow it in. The man who fell among thieves was left half dead, but he was also half alive. It depends on what half of the individual you look at that will determine if you will use your towing power.

CHAPTER 13

Mess Among the Ministerial Ranks

Throughout this book I have expounded on the mess that God's chosen leaders have experienced and are experiencing in dealing with their constituencies. But it would be unfair if I did not lift up and out the mess that exists among the ranks of the clergy. There is a serious chasm within the ecclesiastical family that is threatening the effectiveness of our ministry. Some of the mess that we ministers encounter from the laity is instigated and fueled by some among our ranks. Some of us do some ungodly things to other ministers that bring shame upon the very church we are representing. I would be the first to admit that we all have faults. But when people can see our faults without the use of a "microscope," we are in serious trouble.

One of the main causes of so much mess among us is jealousy. Jealousy is so deeply rooted in some of us that it is destroying our confidence. I don't understand some of the reasons for our jealousy. If we as ministers would utilize our precious time which God has given us, doing what we are called to do, there would not be any time to feel jealous. Some of the jealousy that exists is caused by those toward whom the jealousy is directed. Let's be honest: some of us who are better educated than others will sometimes go out of our way to flaunt our achievements. Some of us wear them on our shirt sleeves while others display them by the way they socialize. There are those who feel left out and unimportant when they are confronted with these kinds of people.

This is not a reason for their jealousy, but it is a cause. In my opinion education prepares us to be able to meet and greet people on all levels without making anyone uncomfortable. Even in some of our meetings, the seating tells the story. Some of us are intoxicated with self. There is nothing more destructive than an intoxicated self. Nebuchadnezzar became intoxicated with himself. We can tell this by the destructive monologue he gave one morning when he walked out on his veranda.

> Is not this great Babylon that I have built for the house of the kingdom by the might of my power, and the honor of my majesty? Dan. 4:30

While he was speaking, God took away his intoxication. He was driven to live and eat with the beasts of the field; his hair grew like eagles' feathers; his nails grew like bird claws. This is what happened to his personality. Nobody wants to be around us when we become intoxicated with ourselves. It turns people off and makes some weak minds feel inferior.

On the other hand, people may feel unimportant and left out because they may have a "grasshopper complex." Listen to these words of the typical "grasshopper":

> And there we saw giants, the sons of Anak
> which come of the giants, and we were in our
> sight as grasshoppers, and so we were in their
> sight. Num. 13:13

These men were sent out to spy on the land so that they might be able to bring back information to help them conquer the land. But after seeing the giant inhabitants of that land, some of the spies felt small. We must keep in mind that the Anaks were people who had long necks. But it is what happened to these spies inside that made them feel like grasshoppers.

There are some giants among us, academically, and there are those who take on the grasshopper complex when we are around them. It is very important how we see ourselves. Either of the above, to the extreme, can be dangerous. What do we see when we stand in front of the mirror? That is the question.

Some ministers are jealous over the size of congregations that others may have. Many of us have been duped into beliving that the size of membership determines our success. But how do we measure success? One important factor is that we assume the larger the congregation, the larger the salary. And in a sense that is true. But if we cannot handle a pig, what do we expect to do with a hog? If we cannot, or will not preach to twenty-five, what is it that makes us think we can preach to twenty-five hundred? Some years ago, President Woodrow Wilson said in an address that "a minister must be something before he can do anything." That is, the character and person are greater than his/her work.

There is another serious problem among us that causes so much mess, and that is the problem of greed. Greed is destroying the credibility of the ministry. I am the first to acknowledge that no organization can survive without money.

But when money becomes our goal, it diminishes all other responsibilities we may have. The question is, How much is enough? Some of us are so preoccupied with the effort of seeing how much is in it for us that we do not spend enough time finding out how much is in us for them. Greed of filthy lucre has caused many clergymen to fall over the past years, especially when there was no need. It is ungodly to "milk" people out of their earnings for the sake of supporting our lavish living and habits. Greed is a cancer that is eating away the basic moral fibers of the ecclesiastical family. If we are truly called and chosen by God, there is no need for us to use most of God's precious time scheming for ourselves. Listen to what David had to say:

> I have been young, and now am old; yet have I not seen the righteous forsaken, nor his seed begging bread. Ps. 37:25

God would never permit his chosen leaders to be in want.

Our society is so complex that it offers a great challenge to the clergy. It bids us to come out of the arena of narrow-mindedness, put away petty jealousies and greed, and confront the major issues faced by members of the church and community. The fact that we wear clerical collars, or are referred to as "Reverend, Minister or Doctor" will not suffice. If we are to serve the present age, we must emphasize life before death as well as life after death. We must expand the horizons of our ministry to include not only the mess but also the "mess up." We must be concerned not only about debit but the derelicts as well.

If we were to put aside our involvement with the mess

and broaden our message, it would take us from prayer meetings to civic meetings; from the church board meetings to the school board meetings; from worshipping to watching. To be able to expound eloquently about the plight of Daniel in the lion's den or about the Hebrew boys in the fiery furnance, while failing to realize that some of our parishioners are trapped in present-day dens and furnaces is a classic example of clerical myopia. We do acknowledge that we are different and that there will always be differences. But we must not allow our differences to derail our pursuit to eradicate the forces of evil that seek to destroy humanity. If we are to go the mileage and spread the message, we must put aside the mess.

> Fret not thyself because of evildoers, neither be thou envious against the workers of iniquity. For they shall soon be cut down like grass, and wither as the green herb. Psalm 37:1-2

Mileage and Mess in Marriages

After God made man He placed him in the garden to be a caretaker. Man was forbidden to eat of the "tree of knowledge," but of the others he had open privileges. Too often many of us refer to that tree as an apple tree. This is done out of complete ignorance. No one has any idea what the tree looked like. We do know that man was not to bother that tree. This was man's first "don't."

God was pleased with man and saw that He needed to fulfill his emotional need. God saw that it was not good for man to be alone. So He created all kinds of beasts of the field and fowls of the air to sing, and gave to man a good environment in which to live. But those beasts and fowls were not compatible with man. They were different and could not compensate one another. God had given man a "help meet," a companion who could be a part of him and share his spiritual and emotional life. So God put Adam to sleep and performed the first operation. He took a rib from Adam and made Eve. This should not be misunderstood. God was not going to form another being from the dust, so he used Adam and began the reproduction. Adam saw Eve and was pleased. He said, "This is now bone of my bone, and flesh of my flesh; she shall be called Woman because she was taken out of man." Woman was made to be a companion and not a competitor—to protect and not to provoke. Little did Adam know that the very woman he admired would be the one to cause him pain and get him in the mess of his life.

> **Serpent:** Say, Eve, did God tell you not to eat of every tree in this garden?
> **Eve:** God told us we may eat of every tree except the one in the midst of the garden. He told us if we do we will die.
> **Serpent:** Ah, Eve, you won't die if you eat of that tree. You see, Eve, God does not want you to become smart. You will become just as knowledgeable as He is. Go ahead and eat it.

This woman listened to this clever, convincing serpent and went to the tree and saw that it was pleasant to the eye. She ate fruit from the tree and then persuaded Adam:

> **Eve:** Hey Adam! Here, eat some of this fruit. It is really tasty.
> **Adam:** Eve! You know we are not supposed to eat the fruit of that tree.
> **Eve:** Oh, go on and eat it. God told us not to eat of that tree because He wanted to keep us ignorant.
> **Adam:** All right, give it to me.

There is no evidence how long it took Eve to convince Adam to partake of that fruit. But I often wonder why Adam listened to Eve rather than God. God gave them specific instructions not to eat the fruit; if they did they would die. Mankind was destined to live forever. But through disobedience death would become a certainty in the existence of mankind. God gave man a will, and the choice he made was his own. Can you imagine Adam and Eve never having to work hard or worry about their living? But Adam blew it when he listened to Eve and got into all this mess.

After eating of the fruit, the Bible tells us that "their eyes were opened." Their moral and spiritual differences came to be known. After eating the fruit Adam became aware of their differences. Shame became a reality. He saw her naked, and she saw him naked. And they sought out materials to hide their bodies.

The Lord: Adam, where are you?
Adam: I am hiding in the garden.
The Lord: Why are you hiding?
Adam: I am hiding because I am afraid. I am naked.
The Lord: Who told you that you were naked?
Adam: The woman you gave me offered me the fruit of the tree, and I ate it and then realized I was naked.
The Lord: Eve, what did you do?
Eve: The serpent tricked me into eating the fruit.

Adam blamed his disobedience on Eve. Eve blamed hers on the serpent. But the bottom line is that each of us is responsible for our own conduct. And now because of the action of Eve and because Adam listened to Eve, they got the whole human race in a mess. The woman, Eve, who represented motherhood, was condemned to bear children in pain, which meant that previously she was to bear children without any pain or discomfort.

Not only that, the man was given rule over her. At the outset they were to share rulership in the garden. But because of the dreadful act that Eve committed, she forfeited all rights and privileges equal to those of Adam. Adam represented manhood and was condemned to toil and sweat in order to make a living. Adam lost his free ride by virtue of his disobedience to God. Manhood is destined to dig and scratch out his existence in the ground. In other words, he lost his paradise all because of the mess that occurred in the first marriage.

There was another marriage that came to a screeching halt. Here was a man who was perfect and upright and feared God. This man, Job, had seven sons and three daughters. He was rich—just look at what he owned: seven thousand sheep, three thousand camels, five hundred yoke of oxen and five hundred she asses. He was the richest man living at that time. Like rich children of today, Job's sons had feasts at their houses. Each day they would go to different houses until they had visited all seven. Then they sent for their three sisters, and ate and drank with them.

One day there was a conversation between Satan and God:

Lord: Satan, where have you been?
Satan: I have been going here and there, trying to see who I can get to do wrong.
Lord: Have you considered Job, My servant?
Satan: Yes, but You have given him everything. He is surrounded with protection, and he is comfortable. But if You take away that hedge of success, I will make him curse You.
Lord: All right, I am giving you the power to do whatever you wish with all of the things he has.

With the power God had given Satan, he went wild.

Thieves came and took the oxen and asses and murdered the servants. Lightning came and burned up the sheep and those who were tending them. Then the Chaldeans came in three different groups and confiscated the camels and killed more servants. The last straw occurred when a storm arose and blew down the house, killing all the sons and daughters.

All of this did not happen in one day or maybe not in a week. But it did happen. Job was terribly shaken. He took off his mantle, shaved his head, fell prone on the ground and worshipped God. Job realized that his life did not consist of things and possessions, so he made this declaration: "Naked came I out of my mother's womb, and naked shall I return thither; the Lord gave, and the Lord hath taken away; blessed be the name of the Lord" (Job 1:21).

Through all of the tragedies that Job had undergone, he did not sin. What a man of faith he was! Satan was not pleased because he had not succeded. He confronted the Lord again:

Lord: Where have you been, Satan?

Satan: Here and there, seeking who I can get to do wrong.

Lord: Have you considered Job?

Satan: I have taken everything he owned, and yet I can't get him to sin. But I know what will do the trick. Hurt his body. Make him suffer; give him some pain, and I know he will curse You to Your face.

Lord: All right, Satan, he is yours to do what you want with him, but spare his life.

Job's body was covered with boils from head to toe. He was so miserable that he took a broken piece of pottery and scraped himself in a pile of ashes. And here is where the real mess started.

Job's wife: Job! With all that you have been through, the loss of all that you had, and the loss of your children, and now your body covered with nasty boils, why do you still maintain your religious integrity? Why don't you curse God and die?

Job: You talk just like all those other foolish women. When we had everything, and you were enjoying it, you did not sound like this. You are a foolish woman.

Nobody knows how long Job was sick. But it is this writer's opinion that Job's wife became impatient with him after a period of time. She got tired of waiting on him and seeing him still hold fast to his faith. Like many people today whose spouses become ill, she grew impatient and disgusted. Job's wife wanted him to curse God, get it over with and die. In her eyes Job did not have anything to live for. I am almost certain that she was going to leave him at the very time she was needed. What a mess of a marriage.

If there is such a thing as an "odd couple," it was the marriage of Ahab and Jezebel. Ahab was one of the strongest and most influential kings of Israel. He was successful in many military conflicts. He commanded two thousand chariots and ten thousand men. He possessed more military equipment than any other king. But Ahab did evil in the sight of the Lord. Ahab's evilness escalated when he thought it would be politically advantageous to marry Jezebel. And maybe it was, but it also proved to be religiously disastrous. You see, Jezebel introduced idolatrous worship of Baal into Israel.

Ahab, like many of us today, was not content with what he had. Ahab wanted a vineyard so he could plant a garden. He went to Naboth to make a deal.

Ahab: Naboth! Give me your vineyard. I need it for a garden.

Naboth: King Ahab, I don't want to lose my inheritance.

Ahab: I need that property. I will give you a larger piece of property somewhere else. Not only that, I will also pay you whatever price you ask.

Naboth: I won't sell.

Ahab: Just name your price, and I will pay it.

Naboth: This property was handed down to me by my father, and I will not let it go.

Ahab was furious and went into the house sulking. Jezebel saw Ahab in a foul mood and wanted to know what his problem was.

Jezebel: Ahab! What is wrong with you that you are in such a bad mood?

Ahab: I want that vineyard next door, but Naboth won't let me have it.

Jezebel: Why are you sitting around here sulking. You are the governor. You can have whatever you want. Stop worrying. I will get that property for you. Just leave it to me.

Jezebel was a cunning woman. She conspired to have Naboth charged with false crimes and even recruited false witnesses to testify against him. The end result was the stoning of Naboth. The sins of Ahab were deferred to his offspring. Ahab was killed in a battle by an arrow in his back. How ironic that is. The death of Jezebel is beyond description. She was thrown down in the streets, and a chariot ran over her; the dogs ate her body. She died a gruesome death. What a mess that marriage was.

As Ahab did, many of us marry for the wrong reason. As we put in the mileage in our marriages, we send mixed messages. And because we overlook the main ingredient of marriage—love—we get ourselves into messes that we regret. Ahab married for political reasons. Although he did evil in the sight of the Lord before he married, at least he was not worshipping idol gods. Jezebel was a strong, domineering woman, and at all costs she was going to get that vineyard for Ahab. We could say without reservation that Ahab and Jezebel were unequally yoked.

CHAPTER 15

Grapes From the Vine

Thou wilt keep him in perfect peace whose mind is stayed on thee: because he trusteth in thee. Isaiah 26:3

Maintaining a Peaceful Mind in a Turbulent World

With all of the murders, robberies, rapes, thefts and other crimes of violence occurring today, how is it possible to maintain a peaceful mind? No person whose mind is stayed on God could possibly rape, murder, steal, abuse or batter another human. Good and evil cannot be housed together. We know that the absence of God means the presence of evil thoughts.

Each of us was born with a clean slate. Everything we do, and every act we commit is learned. All of us are born in a state of innocence; we learn and practice how to be guilty. God is peace, God is love, God is fulfilling, and God will keep you in perfect peace if you keep your mind on Him.

Prayer: Father God, Christ we praise Thee in the midst of tribulations. We submit our minds to You so that we may be at peace with ourselves. Let our minds be as that in Your son, Jesus. May we forever think the good thought. This we ask in Your name. Amen.

I have no greater joy than to hear that my children walk in truth. 3 John 1:4

By Their Parents Ye Shall Know Them

All parents are teachers; all parents are character builders. Parents are not only teachers and character builders, they are also religious instructors, and they stand as examples of Christian principles. The family is the foundation for democracy. When the family unit breaks down, the nation breaks down as well. When children are conceived, they must be nurtured and nourished. No parent desires for his children to become criminals. But it does happen because of negligence and over-protection. The blood of our children be upon our hands.

Prayer: Dear God, give us this day our daily bread— that bread which gives us the substance and fortitude to rear our children in the fear of God. If we falter, let it be from the head and not from the heart. Amen.

For all have sinned, and come short of the glory of God; Being justified freely by his grace through the redemption that is in Christ Jesus. Romans 3:23-24

It Happened at the Cross

Evil has such a stranglehold on human life that none of us can save ourselves. God alone saves. God does not condone sin, but He will not abandon us, because He loves us. Because of God's love for us, He bears the punishment for our sins. It was at the cross that we understood the magnitude of the love of God. We should never lose sight of the glory of our new lives in Christ.

Prayer: Father, in Christ we give thanks for the love You have shown toward us in that You gave Your life for us while we were yet sinners. We pray that You will look mercifully upon us and continue to bless us in spite of our disobedience and shortcomings. Amen.

> Train up a child in the way he should go; and when he/she is old, he/she will not depart from it. Proverb 22:6

Wanted: Good Parents

The result of the lack of training in the home is seen in the crime that rages in our streets and communities. Freud taught that the foundation of character is established by age three. He held that while events may be able to modify, they can never basically alter the traits already formed.

Every aspect of the working world requires testing and training. But there is no device available to measure whether or not those who apply for a license to be married are prepared to be good parents. What this society needs is parents who will be as diligent in seeing that their children go to Sunday school and church as they are in getting them to school every day. They should be as concerned about their children's spiritual development as they are about their social and physical status. If parents love their children as they say they do, they will practice home worship with the family and see that their children know and love the Lord. Any time a nation or people overlook the instructions of God, they are headed for disaster.

Prayer: Our heavenly Father, we pray that Thou will grant us the wisdom so that we may teach our children to grow up to be good men and women. Give us strength to help them to recognize in us and from us the fact that Christianity is a religion of joy, satisfaction and happiness. Amen.

> But ye shall receive power, after that the Holy Ghost is come upon you: and ye shall be witnesses unto me both in Jerusalem, and in all Judaea, and in Samaria and unto the uttermost part of the earth. Acts 1:8

A Witnessing Community

Can you imagine what our communities would be like if every believer took the opportunity to witness for Christ? The New Testament speaks to the church concerning its role in witnessing to the community. The church is a community within a community. Those who have had a personal experience with Jesus Christ, and those who have an unflinching trust in God through Christ, are compelled and obligated to become witnesses.

The church is comprised of "Spirit-filled" members who must work toward creating a "Spirit-filled" community. Witnessing is much more than endless talking. We witness through fellowshipping, worshipping, teaching and through stewardship.

Prayer: My gracious God, You have left us Thy holy Word to be a lamp unto our feet and a light unto our path.

We do humbly pray for You to give unto us all Thy Holy Spirit, so that we may learn what is Thy blessed will. And help us to frame our lives so that we may bring light to our communities. Amen.

See then that ye walk circumspectly, not as fools, but as wise. Ephesians 5:15

Maintaining Spiritual Discipline

Even animals are disciplined in their environment. We, who are intelligent beings, must maintain certain basic spiritual disciplines to be controlled by the love of Christ. The role of the Christian today is the same as it was in Paul's time. To surrender to God, to know Him and to love Him are the only ways we can maintain discipline in our lives. Despite our environment, it is possible for us to be so disciplined that there is always an inner center of quiet discipline. We must be disciplined in prayer, study and worship. We must also constantly evaluate ourselves in order to know where we are falling short.

Prayer: Father of the universe and Creator of mankind, give us the strength we need to maintain the attitude and conduct of a Christian life. In the midst of turmoil, give us love that will constrain and sustain us each day of our lives, so that we may be beacons for the world to see. Amen.

And ye shall know the truth, and the truth shall make you free. John 8:32

Free to Do What?

We must first acknowledge that there are two types of freedom: freedom to do whatever you want, and freedom to do what you ought. All over the world men and women are fighting, dying and crying for their freedom. Even those who are enjoying "freedom" are crying for more freedom. Freedom to do what? Freedom is more than the absence of bars and shackles. Freedom is having the inward resources to cope with outward restraints. Freedom is never free. Every freedom that you now enjoy was made possible by a sacrifice of others. There must be sacrifices made in order to boast of being free. With freedom comes responsibilities. God said to Pharoah, "Let My people go, that they may serve Me." No matter how free you think you are, you are not completely free until you acknowledge that God is. Many of us are prisoners to bad habits and hang-ups. Freedom is not a physical thing; it is a spiritual state. It is a state of mind.

Prayer: Most gracious Father, we praise Thee for the freedom of Your Spirit. Give us the strength to proclaim to the world that we are free because through Your Son, the Truth, we have been set free. Teach us not to trust in our own wisdom and strength, but to submit wholly to the presence of Your wisdom and Spirit. This we ask in the name of Jesus. Amen.

References used in the writing of this book:

Cruden's Complete Concordance; 1968 by Zondervan
    Publishing House
The Abingdon Bible Commentary; 1929 by Abingdon
    Press, Inc.
The Zondervan Pictorial Bible Dictionary; 1967 by
    Zondervan Publishing House

Strength

Not unto him comes strength who sits
With folded hands where flames are warm,
And hopes that God will come between
Him and the fury of the storm.
But unto him alone comes strength
Who prays for strength to face the blast,
Until the night be spent and he
Beholds the rising sun at last

Ines Clark Thorson

To order additional copies of *The Mileage, The Message and The Mess* or to contact Nolan T. Pitts to speak to your group write:

Nolan T. Pitts
P.O. Box 2111
Eatonville, FL 32751
(407) 644-5985 or
(407) 323-3014